PRICKS

IN

THE

TAPESTRY

PRICKS

IN THE

TAPESTRY

JAMESON FITZPATRICK

Birds, LLC
Minneapolis, New York, Raleigh

Birds, LLC
Minneapolis, New York, Raleigh
www.birdsllc.com

Cover art: Paul Thek
Sea Series 1975
enamel on newspaper
22 3/4 x 33 1/4 in/58 x 84 cm
photo: Joerg Lohse
©Estate of George Paul Thek, Courtesy Alexander and Bonin, New York
Cover design by Zoe Norvell
Interior photo on title page by William Karam
Interior design by Zoe Norvell

Library of Congress Cataloging-in-Publication Data:
Fitzpatrick, Jameson
Pricks in the Tapestry / Jameson Fitzpatrick

First Edition, 2020
ISBN: 978-0-9826177-2-4
Printed in the Untied States of America

Contents

for my grandmothers, the poets

Scintilla, Star

In the old place, there was no place
that did not see me.
Wherever I went mothers whispered
about me like a Greek chorus:
"I heard that boy…" I heard that.
I was just a boy. But it was
true, what they said, that I liked
other boys, that I had stolen Sarah's,
though he was four years older
and they were very much in love.
I made him break up with her
in a Chili's parking lot
while I waited inside. I was
fourteen. How humbling
to have been fourteen, to have eaten
at that Chili's, often. That summer
I had no taste for anything
but him. Faintly of chlorine.
When he left for college
I had no one. Sarah's friends
stared me down at school.
I found it was better,
if I could not be no one,
to be someone. Small, but
particular. Specified, which was
an apprenticeship for special.
Cold, another word for cool.

The Last Analysis; or, I Woke Up

and it was political.
I made coffee and the coffee was political.
I took a shower and the water was.
I walked down the street in short shorts and a Bob Mizer tank top
and they were political, the walking and the shorts and the beefcake
silkscreen of the man posing in a G-string. I forgot my sunglasses
and later, on the train, that was political,
when I studied every handsome man in the car.
Who I thought was handsome was political.
I went to work at the university and everything was
very obviously political, the department and the institution.
All the cigarettes I smoked between classes were political,
where I threw them when I was through.
I was blond and it was political.
So was the difference between "blond" and "blonde."
I had long hair and it was political. I shaved my head and it was.
That I didn't know how to grieve when another person was killed in America
was political, and it was political when America killed another person,
who they were and what color and gender and who I am in relation.
I couldn't think about it for too long without feeling a helplessness
like childhood. I was a child and it was political, being a boy
who was bad at it. I couldn't catch and so the ball became political.
My mother read to me almost every night
and the conditions that enabled her to do so were political.
That my father's money was new was political, that it was proving something.
Someone called me faggot and it was political.
I called myself a faggot and it was political.
How difficult my life felt relative to how difficult it was
was political. I thought I could become a writer

and it was political that I could imagine it.
I thought I was not a political poet and still
my imagination was political.
It had been, this whole time I was asleep.

Sometimes I See a Man Who Hurts Me

Just the fact of the size of him.
Any him.
How much he doesn't struggle to fill.
The broadness of shoulders that in no sense belong to me.
Shoulders I can neither have nor climb.
If that isn't cruelty.
How they cut through the air and what else.
The way the fabric pulls across.
The way the sleeve hangs open when he reaches up.
The way the armpit calls me to memorize it.
The way he must lower the arm.
The way the bicep twitches.
The way the back ripples.
The way the ankle peeks.
The way the band of underwear inches upward
so he must reach in to push himself down again.
The scratch while he's there.
The way there is no anguish in the face.
The way he looks in any direction, away from me.

Selected Boys: 2003–2008

boys in the woods   beating off   off the beaten   between the barn and sandpit
seemed bigger once   with their pants down   around their ankles   boys
leaning against trees   rubbing up against trunks   boys raw   boys wiping up
with leaves   boys in bathrooms   at school   in class   boys in tights   boys in
dance belts   boys backstage   during the show   boys after hours   in empty
studios   boys in cars   taking off   not wearing seatbelts   taking off their
belts   boys in back seats   boys in front seats   boys in trunks   boys swimming
half naked   across the pond or pool or summer   skimming stones   boys
streaking   starlike through the dark   boys in basements   boys sprouting   hair
in all the places parts come together   boys coming together   boys leaving
separately   15 minutes apart   then meeting in the park   boys getting drunk
boys getting stoned   boys getting blown   boys fucking raw   boys like Jack
Dave   Brandon   Justin   John   Chris   Mike   Daniel   Mark   Matt   Drew
Mark again   Brian   Zack   Kevin   Josh   Nick   who died   who's counting

The Last Time I Got [ ]

I only let him
because he was sort of famous
and I wanted to say I had.

And the time before that,
because he was sort of straight
and I wanted to have my say—

and before that,
because he was there,
and he was going to.

Once Jacques got in,
where I wanted him,
but not all the way

and I wouldn't let him
move it, I just
finished myself off and burst

into tears. It was fine,
I was fine, it was just a lot,
what Lot wouldn't let

his neighbors do
to the angels. And he didn't
even know they were angels.

Lot has nothing to do
with it, why I won't.
Or can't, if will isn't the thing.

But isn't the mind the body.
Isn't mine. And what has
been done to it, and how:

plucked like a flower
versus
plucked like a string.

Poem in Which Nothing Bad Ever Happens to Me

I make the train.
And get the job
and pay my rent on time
and don't get too drunk and don't
send the text and always use a condom.

The car does not make an illegal left turn and I do not have to brake hard to
avoid it and I do not fly off my bike and flip several feet in the air and I do
not land thinking *not on my face not on my face* hard on my right arm and I do
not break my elbow and a mean orthopedist does not tell me I have to move
it anyway or risk losing my range of motion and I do not have to teach while
on Percocet which is harder and less fun than you might imagine.

None of my friends ever kill themselves.

I never even meet one of them, because I'm never admitted to a psychiatric
hospital, because I never want to kill myself, or say I will, or gesture to
repeatedly in order to prevent someone from abandoning me, which, I'll never
learn, is what a therapist I'll never meet refers to as a "communication tactic."

In this poem, I don't even fear abandonment.

Jacques never leaves me, or, I never meet Jacques.

Or we fuck once, or we fuck a few times
but love never enters the building.
Love, in this case, is the bad thing,
or the absence of kindness in the face of love;
so in this poem, wherever there is love
there will be kindness and where there is no kindness
there will be no love.

I don't hate the feeling of a man inside me, or, there are never any men inside me in this poem.

Another man with a French name I love never pushes me down into the cold concrete of a stairwell and fucks me dry, without a condom. If he fucks me at all, it is tenderly, in an expensive hotel where I do not learn to like it again because I never stopped.

I never offer to suck the dick of the boy I am sharing a hotel room with on a high school trip and he never insists on fucking me and I never say yes and I never say "stop" or can't remember whether or not I do and this question does not haunt me because it never happens.

When I'm sixteen, a middle-aged man next to me at the theater does not touch my knee and it does not terrify me how much I like it.

I'm never a teenager at all, if it can be arranged. I see the car coming and don't make the left turn.

My parents never:
keep booze in the house,
name me after it.

There's still pot in this poem, but I smoke less of it.

I don't have to keep stopping and starting
to get high and masturbate; this poem pours out of me, easy,
like conversation with strangers at a bar, even when I'm sober,
which I might be sometime at one of the bars in this poem.

There's nothing I don't want to write
about. I love writing.

I love my body.

I'm not gay in this poem, or it is not hard to be gay in this poem. Stet—it's been useful, because it's been hard.

But not *so* hard, I'm not forced to come out in the sixth grade, at least—not to my parents, because I never get reported for writing something obscene about Justin Timberlake on an AOL message board, and not to everyone else, because it isn't so apparent to them already.

In middle school, none of the boys ever follow me around in the hallway between classes, lisping. I don't have a crush on one of them and he doesn't ask me out as a joke one day when everyone is hanging out by the picnic tables before school and I don't find myself somehow relieved that I know it's a joke the whole time because falling for it would have been way worse.

Phil Bruno doesn't write an essay for AP English our senior year of high school which is both a personal attack on me and on gay people more generally. He doesn't read it aloud in front of the entire class and the teacher doesn't let him finish and I don't gather my things and walk out. If he does, and I do, I don't walk straight out of the school without stopping to look at anyone, I go to the principal's office and raise hell and maybe make a YouTube video about it that I parlay into some small fame. I don't feel embarrassed about how many times I've let him copy my math homework.

In this poem, I get revenge
only on the people who owe it
to me, who is no one.

On Halloween, when I'm nine, the co-pilot of a Boeing 767 en route to Cairo does not crash the plane into the Atlantic Ocean sixty miles south of Nantucket, just into international waters. If he does, my father's parents aren't on board. The US authorities never determine that the co-pilot seized the controls, did it on purpose, but can't explain why. There's not a second, conflicting investigation, because the Mubarak government doesn't insist this isn't true. I never know my father as the child this happens to.

Two years later, I don't ejaculate for the first time at summer camp, at the hands of a boy who is a year or two older, who I didn't know before this summer but knew of because he'd gotten kicked out of my elementary school for bringing in a beebee gun. I don't pretend to be asleep the whole time because I am afraid of him but also afraid

I don't want him to stop. I don't tell
our counselors the next day because I don't know
how to feel about it but recognize it as familiar,
the first bad thing that was done to me, and now
neither of us can stay. I don't feel guilty about this, for years.

And the first bad thing,
much further back than that,
is not my first memory, or
what I understand to be the first
because over time I have
smoothed and perfected it
like a stone in my palm.

Here my hands are empty.
Here it never happens, so I don't have to tell you about it.

Duplicity

Whenever I am in one conversation
I am thinking about another.
Whatever room I am in my heart is not.
Before a mirror, which face is true:
the one that moves or the one that is moved?
I flip a coin and wish for the opposite.
Life, friends, is whoring.
A warning a man mistakes for intimacy.
When I miss my madness, which I mostly don't,
I miss how totally I was inside it,
the idea I could not get out.

Frantic Efforts to Avoid Abandonment, Real or Imagined

Once I wove flowers into his bicycle spokes.

I wrote PLEASE on the wall in large letters.

I wrote letters.

Many times I made a scene.

Once I cast a spell.

I told him I could keep him beautiful.

I chased after him in the street, calling his name.

I was always It.

I showed up at the party knowing he would be there and went home with him.

I showed up at the party not knowing he would be there and went home with him.

I texted twice more after it was clear he didn't want to sleep with me again.

I learned about sympathetic magic in class, then got his signature tattooed on my ass.

I followed him onto the subway platform.

I followed him on every platform.

I told him I would die without him.

I died.

That was the worst thing.

No, coming back was the worst thing.

Haunting him.

I wore a disguise.

Sang the Stevie Nicks song right in his face.

You'll never get away from the sound of the woman that loves you.

I paid for it.

Slept with his friend.

Several of them.

Claimed squatter's rights.

I waited by the door.

I wrapped my arms around him.

I turned him into a tree.

I climbed.

Carved our initials into the bark.

I jumped.

Where I landed I didn't know the language.

I repeated his name in a mirror until he appeared.

I broke the mirror trying to get to him.

I broke two.

I turned him into a flower.

I turned him into a pig.

I cooked him breakfast.

I did the dishes.

I learned the language.

I devised a plot.

I devised a plot of such sophistication he'd never suspect.

I stole his passport.

I made everyone he loved love me.

Once I told the truth about everything.

I lied.

I was extravagant.

I was simple.

I was a good piece of furniture.

I was his favorite shirt.

A True Account of Overhearing Andy Cohen at Fire Island

His voice woke me this afternoon loud
and queer on the beach, saying "You
can have a glass of rosé at lunch"—
I missed the rest but opened my eyes
in time to see him strolling there
through the surf with his dog

                    and two
younger men, tanned and toned
but still boyish in their appeal, nearly
identical in their woven straw hats
though one a little shorter

                 and the brim
of one hat wider than the other.

I know the dog's name because I follow him
on Instagram (the man, not the dog)
as I wanted to follow him then

                 down the beach
calling—what? "Excuse me, Mr. Cohen,
I've been having a crisis of confidence
approximately since birth so I was
wondering if I might join you on your walk
along the water, as I've got a feeling
everything would change for me
if I were the kind of person people spotted
with Andy Cohen in the Pines. I might
get a TV deal! Or believe the men
who find me attractive."

               That would be
crazy, of course. I'd look ridiculous

in one of those hats.
                    They got smaller
and smaller, the famous man and the two
younger in triangle formation behind him
with the dog darting in between. I was left
with my large hangover and too-small
towel and the solace that
                              to the average
eye I almost resemble them, the younger men
I shouldn't assume are sleeping with him.

But I know better. The difference of the hats,
for instance. They're easy in a way
I'll never be—not as in sex, not
as in easily won, I mean they move
in their bodies through space
with the ease of winners, naturals
at being—
            being
being my biggest problem, followed by
love and attention in roughly that order.
Sex too, but I used to be better at it.
But too early. Money I was always bad at.

Last night I took half a tab hoping to get some
advice from the ghost of Frank O'Hara
or at least the moon but all I got was lost
by Jacques at the underwear party
and too anxious
                  to get it up
in the backroom's sea of bodies,
the whole scene dazzling me
                              like the sun
I couldn't get too close or look
too long. I could never fathom

pleasure without hardship,
how men can take it in each other
so effortlessly. Effortlessness as it happens
is what my poems have lacked but

                                         genuinely
if I've got anything going for me it's
my difficulty.

                    That's enough, Jameson.
You may not be the greatest thing
on earth
            or on this beach.
Other voices might be calling to you,
but they're calling you all the same.

Short Essay on the Lyric-Conceptual Divide

All opinions are the speaker's of the poem. Appropriations ≠ endorsements.

Everything that happens in the poem happens to me but the me is not me or rather it is not I though I may have been me in the past.

This poem will contain an image, the value of which I will assert either by virtue of itself or of its context.

A long-armed teenager bites his lip, on a loop, so that he is never not biting his lip or about to bite his lip or having just bitten his lip.

This image is either interesting or it is not.

If it is interesting, it is because it interests the artist and/or the audience.

If I am the artist and it interests me, the boy is a stranger or is known to me.

If he is a stranger, I took this image either with or without consent, or the only extent to which I have taken this image is from someone else who took it first, that is, from the internet.

If he is known to me he is either known intimately or barely.

If he is known barely, he may be a stranger, the image of whom I took with his consent, thereby he became less strange to me, or he may look familiar because his face is a famous face featured in a proliferation of images.

If he is known intimately, I may or may not have once slept with him. If I have not slept with him, he may or may not be a virgin.

He may be a poet. If he is not, he may or may not have aspirations of being a poet.

He may not be a poet.

If he is my first real lover from high school, now dead, this has become a confessional poem. If the gif does not exist, this is a fiction.

After seven months of sobriety, his longest ever, the drug took hold of him again. Through everything, his family never stopped believing in him and loving him and only wish that he could have believed in himself. To all of you who are facing this horrible scourge as the family or friend of an addict, please reach out every day and be there for him or her. Let them know how much you love them and that there is nothing they could do to lose that love. To all of you who are addicted, never give up. A slip-up isn't a failure, and you don't ever have to be ashamed.

The boy bites his lip. Again.

Strawberries

Hickey I did not leave there
And where did I last
on whose neck

Hickey that did not happen
Mistake I did not make
Fuck me it wasn't me

Eye taking notes
Eye taking note of
Hickeys eye cannot look away from
red cluster around which green
I satellite

Pity the young man rising
already older by the end of the hour

Sundays he pays for the pleasure
like a gentleman

I Don't Know Why, It Makes Me Sad

I don't know why
it makes me sad
to meet a man
in the last stall
of the sixth floor
men's room, on a
Saturday, so no one
is around. No hello
but our cocks out
and the goodbad
smell of him, whiff
of piss. I don't
know why it makes
me sad, his dirty
t-shirt and his ring,
the labored grunt
before he cums.
I don't know how
(it makes me sad)
when it is over
he tucks himself
back into his life
unchanged.

Oh,

What did you look like
when they pulled you from the river?
Were you shirtless again?

Remember the afternoon we kept
like a private joke, what we tried and failed?
Does this poem fail you?

Does it keep you alive
in the sunny spot on the floor
where you went to lie

like a dog when you left the bed?
Come here, you said. I'm sorry.
Come here anyway and let me hold you.

From a Friend

I hear you loved me.
You never said.
But knowing one person
has come to this conclusion
is enough—not my friend
but another man she knows
you slept with. When you
go, take my longing with you.
I have no use for it now.

Pierced

Like desires I could not keep track of.
One I left on the estate, in the house

Breuer built: a painted turquoise stud
on the bedside table. The last I lost

in church, if you can believe it, mid-
reading: the tiny triangle loosed itself

from my lobe, its back clinging on
clueless. The silver hoop I mistook

for mine and borrowed from your
drawer—who knows whose or where?

Someplace in a heap of medical waste,
my first (an infection) is buried.

Several of many crosses forgotten in
strange rooms, on damp windowsills,

sly evangelists winking in the sun.
I wondered if a diamond could make

me careful, but the lesson was more
than I could afford. Lately I've taken

to going without, not bothering,
so that in every mirror a conundrum

greets me: that whatever I use to fill
the hole I lose. Or that I put it there,

that it would close if I could let it—

Grasping at Being Filled

Fill me, O Muse   fill
    all my holes   my holes
there are so many of them
I look like St. Sebastian
there is the first hole   the hole
from when I was born
dragged kicking-screaming into
this world   this world
is a hole   there is the second hole
the absence of   the father
the relative absence of   every father absent in his own way
you can count on it like a
rhyme   rhyme
or
fact   the fact that in a certain pair of shorts
I'll get looks from men
anywhere I go   different looks
depending on the neighborhood
there it goes
the third hole
when I got touched
but not where
I got touched   and the fourth hole
the hole of sexual difference
the hole of childhood
then the hole of
the end of childhood   the end of childhood
in the backseat of Dave's Saturn
the hole of being fourteen   and the hole of him
leaving for college
the hole of being stuck
queer in a small town   forever

forever   the hole of the feeling of forever
of not being able to drive yet
the hole left by every crush that followed
the hole of what did or did not happen
the hole one made of me in that hotel

the hole of having to
go on like this
the deep hole of my voice   womanly but not quite
not quite manly   hole of not-quite
hole of in-between
hole of my inability to
get fucked   fucked
I mean seriously
hole of my actual hole   the joke of which I am the butt
hole of the failure to fulfill   the desires of men which are
the expectations of men
in this country
hole of this country   holes this country has made
but
back to me
hole of narcissism
hole of neuroticism
hole of ego   hole of I
hole of my mind
from which nothing   not I
escapes
hole I made
when I threw   what was it
whatever it was
hole of Jacques's face   when I did it
hole of guilt
hole of shame

hole of my lack of compassion   for myself
hole of energy
wasted wanting to die   wanting to die
when dying is the only thing
you can't fuck up

hole of my week in the psych ward
hole of my dead friends
the hole   made in the water   when he jumped
the hole   made in the street   when she jumped
the hole   made in my love   when he OD'd
hole of what I didn't get to say
hole of the illusion it would have made   a difference
hole of how I miss them
hole of being ruled by pettier concerns   petty concerns
my "career"
my booklessness
my endowment
why people never remember me

hole of the incredible smallness
of my problems
pinpricks   pricks
in the infinite tapestry
of all that is fucked up
hole of the news   every day
hole of the everyday
how it dulls
how the hole bores
hole of the light shining through
hole of light and how its beauty
accomplishes nothing   nothing but
the hole of beauty
God   please fuck my mind for good
like John Giorno said
dissolve it
into absolute equanimity

                              void me
                              let me be
like a water glass
                              whole
            if I'm full   whole
            if I'm empty

Roughly

Imagine ~a door.
C-C chemokine receptor type 5 (CCR5) is the protein on the surface of white blood cells through which HIV typically enters.

Imagine ~a locked door.
CCR5 Δ32 is a deletion mutation of this protein resulting in no functional CCR5 receptors on cell surfaces. The ~1% of the European population who is homozygous for the CCR5 Δ32 allele is resistant to M-tropic HIV-1 infection, even in the face of multiple high-risk exposures.

Imagine ~a jammed door.
The ~10% of the European population heterozygous for CCR5 Δ32 has a >50% reduction of functional CCR5 receptors on cell surfaces, relative to people without the mutation (known as the "wild type"), resulting in greater resistance to HIV-1 infection relative to wild types and, when infected, reduced viral loads, a 2–3-year slower progression to AIDS and improved virological response to antiviral drugs—again, relative to wild types.

My hypothesis is this:

Based on our ancestry and how long he lived after contracting HIV at the time that he did, I believe my uncle might have been heterozygous for CCR5 Δ32.

My method is not scientific.

~

Some background:

Christopher was born in New Jersey in 1955. When he was thirteen, he left home for six years.[1] The circumstances surrounding his running away remain unclear to me.[2] In the earliest version of this story I can remember hearing, he was simply missing until he wasn't, reappearing one day in 1974 at age nineteen. Later I'd learn he'd needed surgery. As my grandmother told it, or as I heard it told, this was how she found out both that he was gay[3] and about

---

My Mother's Notes

1   I believe he ran away for 3 years, at age 16. He did steal my parents' car (possibly at age 13, 14, or 15)—before he had a learner's permit or driver's license and drove all the way from NJ to the Delaware Water Gap. I think the police called and both my parents drove to Delaware to drive the two cars and Christopher home. Pretty sure he "went" to Pingry (it was a private boys day school at that time) until he was 16. Apparently he skipped a lot of school. My parents found out he had been taking the train from Red Bank—not to the Pingry station-stop, but into NYC. I remember very tense dinners until he left. Shortly before he returned home, he made a very fancy dinner for Mom, Dad, and me—maybe there were other guests there—I think there were. At any rate, at that time I was told that he had been working at a restaurant in Asbury Park, which is where he learned to make the delicious blue cheese salad dressing he served us and a few of the other things he made. I only remember the salad dressing. I don't remember my parents talking to me about his leaving. If I asked about him, which I imagine I would have, they clearly reassured me that he was okay. They persuaded him to come home and agreed to send him to "hairdressing school." He did well there. He had two brushes with the police that first year. One was a traffic accident where he rear-ended the car in front of him, which had apparently stopped short. The police report said my brother said, "I seen the car but I couldn't stop," which either proves he was really shook up or the cop who wrote it didn't speak or write as well as Chris. The other was when he assaulted some jerk in a coffee shop who was verbally abusing him because he was gay. "Assault" really wasn't the right word, because Chris was scrawny and girlish at that age. He didn't know how to punch, nor did he have the heft to injure someone. But he did punch the guy in the face. He came home with a bruised face. I don't know if I am imagining this (the bruises) or whether it's true. I remember being confused that my brother actually punched someone and also proud that he stood up for himself.

2   I was in 4th grade, Chris in 6th, when we moved from CT to NJ. He must've gone to the K–8 school I went to, but I have no memory of it. Or perhaps he took the train to Pingry with Jeff. I remember him having a (female) date to a school dance and my parents being happy about it. I also remember asking him whether he had a good time and him saying no. It was about then (some time in middle school) that he was miserable all the time.

3   I think she knew that he was gay. She had taken him to psychiatrists to find out why he was unhappy. She later told me he bamboozled every one (I think there were only 2) because he was so much smarter than they were.

anal sex.[4] I am skeptical about at least the first part of this claim, because in 2011, ~6 months before she died, she told me something surprising: that she'd known where he was the whole time he was gone.[5] "Some gutters are lined with mink," she said. This altered my prior assumption that he had been hustling on the streets of New York during his time away and led me to suspect that he had, instead, been kept by some rich older man or series of men.[6] I spent a lot of time with my grandmother the summer before she died. It was also that summer, perhaps during this very conversation, that she told me she was the first person[7] in the family who he told he was positive. She kept his status a secret from her husband, his father, until 2005, when an angry friend (and, I assume, lover[8]) of his called my grandfather to inform him.[9] Last summer, while I was visiting my childhood home for my mother's birthday, she showed me a printed copy of the email my uncle had subsequently sent my

---

4   Pretty sure this is true!

5   She told me this in real-time and we once drove to Asbury Park to "lay eyes" on him. We did not succeed.

6   Interesting. I believe early on he was, in fact, a sex worker in Asbury Park. I also believe he was "befriended" by a wealthy gay couple late in his time away.

7   He never told anyone else in the family.

8   I don't know if Chris and Kenny were ever lovers. They bonded over being gay, though, calling each other "girl." Kenny recently Facebook friended me. I can't bring myself to accept. He made my father cry.

9   Actually, Kenny was distraught because Christopher had stopped taking his antiviral medications. I don't know if he knew Dad didn't know, although, if they were such friends, he should have? Kenny wanted Mom and Dad to make Christopher take his meds so he wouldn't die. When in hospice, Chris told me he stopped taking his meds because they made him feel terrible all the time and he was just tired of it. I believe he also did not have the money to pay for his meds at the end. I think Chris told me he had a gay physician who generously gave him free care (and I believe free or discounted drugs). When the physician died, Chris did not have the benefit, nor was he willing to ask for help from Mom and Dad or disclose his secret to other family members who might help. I'm not certain if this is true or imagined—I think he told me this in hospice.

grandfather, which she'd recently found in a box of my grandmother's papers.[10] In this email, he wrote:

"For 25 years, half my life, I have lived ~ flourished even ~ with the most certain of uncertainties. At age 25, I was forced to consider Mortality in an unprecedented fashion; not by War, with it's [sic] heroic undertones, nor by Famine, Drought or other Disaster that randomly wipe out tens of thousands without prejudice, but by a hideously stigmatic and selective disease, not even named at that point. I have lived with this infection from the very beginning. At the beginning, I made a plan.

"There's no good time for bad news, especially about an irreversible situation, and I am proud to say I felt well-equipped and prepared to handle it without bringing sadness as a burden to my family or friends. No one knew what would happen back then. I kept abreast of the emerging supporting science and sought the best available observation and treatment in New York, paying for it out-of-pocket because there was uncertainty about insurance coverage. I confided in no one for several years.

"I planned to live a rich and full life, without pity or shame, and I have. And I continue."

He died thirteen months after sending that email, to the day.[11] There's no good time for bad news, especially about an irreversible situation, but I did not really know him.

~

---

10   My repressive powers are enormous. I had no memory of this email until I read this.

11   Is this true?

Some questions:

Did you ever go to Fire Island?[12]

That's where I'm writing from.

Where did you stay?

Did you ever party at Tommy Tune's house?

I'm catsitting there. Long story.

What did my mom wear when you took her to
Studio 54?[13]

We saw *Cabaret* at the theater that's there now.

Did you have a great love?[14]

How many?[15]

One here. Maybe two.

Did you forgive your parents?[16]

Were you more afraid when you left or when you came
back?

Did you forgive yourself?[17]

---

12   I don't know but somehow I think yes.

13   I wore a dress I bought at Syms. I wore it on my trip to Boulder, CO before I met your Dad, and I also wore it to The Beaver Club in Montreal the 1st night of our honeymoon stay there when Dad came down with the stomach flu. It was a great dress.

14   Jim W. He came to many family holiday celebrations in NJ. Chris broke up with him and Jim followed him to FL. They became good friends. Jim was really, really good to Chris in his last few months. Jim drove me to and from the airport when I went to say goodbye to Chris in hospice.

15   Maybe it was me or maybe it was Mom. But as for romantic relationships, other than Jim I would say no.

16   He never blamed them and always felt supported by them.

17   His email to Dad would suggest yes.

What did you spend the money on?[18]

What would I spend the money on?

Champagne taste.

Where were you?

Not his anymore.

~

In 1989, Christopher won the lottery: $1,378,886, payable over 20 years. Adjusted for inflation, that would be ~$2.5 million today.

The *Asbury Park Press* ran the story with the headline: "Red Bank man wins $1.3 million prize." This is how he describes getting the winning numbers:

"I obviously didn't believe it [...] I had someone else look ever [sic] my shoulder. I got very quiet, and lost all color. I couldn't speak above a whisper for about 24 hours. I really couldn't [...] I put the winning ticket in my wallet for the rest of the afternoon, and then I transferred it to a safe deposit box [...] I was afraid if I kept looking at the ticket the numbers would change."

The article describes him as a licensed beautician, the owner of a local beauty salon, and, until 1985, the weekly social columnist for the paper. A quick search of the library databases at the university where I teach turns up the digitized archives from 1999 on and the microfiche from 1903 to 1974. I don't know what happened to 1975 through 1998.

I'm able to find three of his columns on Google. They are, frankly, boring—accounts of fundraisers and flower arrangements.

---

18   He loved beautiful things in any category, and he had great taste. He had no "money sense" ever. If he had the money, he spent it and then some.

Asked how he planned to spend the money, he said:

"My staff will all get bonuses [...] I have a wonderful staff. They stood by me for the first few years. That's the first thing I'm going to do. [...] I really live very nicely. I'm so embarrassed [...] Now I can live very nicely without looking over my shoulder. [...] I'm a small businessman, and I opened my own business a few years ago, so I have some debts to pay off [...] I'm going to buy a house, do the kinds of things people do when they win the lottery."

By the end of his life, he had gone bankrupt.

~

Did you ever feel lonely in a crowd?
Did you miss them when they were gone?
Was it worse?
Did you leave the TV on just so you wouldn't be
    alone with yourself?
Did it ever overwhelm you—the way the ocean and
    the sky touch endlessly out here, without relief?
Did the rough red moon?
When a handsome man walked by on the beach, did it
    feel like your chest was collapsing in on itself, like it
    could kill you?
Did many handsome men walk by, so that it began to
    feel like this all the time?
Did you ever see a sinkhole in Florida?
I hear there's a lot of them.

~

I don't know how he lost his money.

I know he drank. I know he moved to Daytona Beach and bought a house. I know he had a little dog[19] whose teeth he used to brush. That is my clearest picture of him, the one time we visited: holding the dog in his lap and brushing her teeth with a tiny toothbrush. A comic image.

I think he stopped drinking.[20]

A memory: my parents arguing behind a closed door about how best to help him.

I know when I came out, at twelve, my mother was afraid—of history, its repetitions. She told me as much.[21]

Sitting on the deck of the house where we were vacationing, at thirteen, I promised her I'd have the life she wished for me, a normal life.[22]

It was an unfair promise, and, for her part, an unfair wish.

~

---

19   Sophie! He LOVED that dog.

20   He did not.

21   My memory is that I told you how unhappy Chris was and how his life was made so much more difficult because he was gay. That I wanted for each of my children to have as easy a time in life as possible because it was hard enough without extra challenges. I did not know about his diagnosis until Dad called me crying.

22   I have no memory of this.

Were you a Normal Gay?[23] Was that even a
thing then?
Did you ever see TV stars at tea?

Probably.

But they were closeted back then?

Of course.

Did you spot them in the crowd and then drift
their way to smoke at a respectful distance,
but close enough they might notice you?
Did one of them light up too, and did
it surprise you, because he was a singer, on
Broadway[24] as well as on TV? Did you order
another drink just to have an excuse to keep
standing by? A drink you didn't need?
Did they notice you?

Were you ever lonelier than you were at tea,
alone?

Did you ever go without your glasses,[25] so that
everyone looked like a familiar stranger?

Everything you saw—did you see it softer?
Roughly?

---

23   He built quite a life for himself in Red Bank. Everyone knew he was gay. He was pop-
ular, owned his own business, held elected (or appointed?) office(s), rubbed elbows with the
ultra-rich, and was known for being a perfect host and throwing excellent parties. He lived like
a king on Judy Stanley's Rumson estate (in the carriage house). PS I don't know what "Normal
Gay" means.

24   When I was in high school I went to see *Candide* on Broadway. His neighbor and acquain-
tance was in it. God he was handsome! I tried to get Chris to introduce me but he never did.

25   Chris wore contact lenses for many, many years. And he prided himself on "seeing clear-
ly"—double entendre intended.

Did you like it?

On your way back to the house, did you spot a
     large dog up the boardwalk and mistake it
     for a deer?

~

There are ~300 white-tailed deer on Fire Island according to the National
Park Service website. The Park Service discourages visitors from touching
or feeding them for the protection of both deer and humans alike. Food-
conditioning can change the deer's natural behavior and "lead to undesirable
and potentially unsafe human-deer interactions."

I'm surprised that Lyme disease is not mentioned in this warning, as it has
always come to mind when I have been confronted by the irrefutable cuteness
of the deer off the side of the boardwalk, or on the beach, or resting under the
ramp leading up to the house, looking up at me.

Where I grew up, in a small town in Connecticut, everyone was always worried
about Lyme disease. It seemed that way to me as a child, anyway. Anytime
we came in from playing outside we had to be checked for ticks; when we
got older we had to check ourselves. I remember learning about the signs and
symptoms in Sunday school, awareness was considered so important and the
threat so great. The bull's-eye rash.

It surprises people now—people in my life, I mean—that I grew up in the
woods, or at least so near them. Many of the happier moments of my unhappy
childhood were spent running through trees, pretending to be a nymph or
sprite or otherwise fay nonhuman creature. The cosmopolitan Jameson is
a late invention.

How did the deer get to Fire Island, you might wonder.
I wondered. They walked. Over the ice one winter in the middle of the
19th century.

~

Imagine it's years ago.

More years than that.

Another century.

And another. Keep going.

Cross an ocean.

Then further and farther north.

On my desktop, I keep thirteen windows open, and in each one, multiple tabs. I am trying to keep track of the literature, though I can't follow much past the abstracts.

Bear with me.

Appreciable levels of CC55 Δ32 are only found in European and West Asian populations. The allele's frequency is highest—~14–16%—in Northern Europe, on either side of the Baltic Sea, with a north-south cline. The highest frequency of the homozygous genotype—2.3%—was recorded in the Faroe Islands.

Its distinct distribution pattern and high frequency together suggest that CCR5 Δ32 is the result of a single unique mutation event that occurred sometime after the divergence of Europeans from their African ancestors but before the emergence of HIV in the early 20th century, and that the gene was then subject to positive selection—meaning the mutation was good for something. What it was good for remains a topic of scientific debate.

The prevailing hypothesis was once that the current frequency of CCR5 Δ32 could be attributed to the so-called Black Death, which killed ~one-third of the European population in the middle of the 14th century. People with the mutation survived, the story goes, and passed it on. But the Black Death is believed to have been a pandemic of bubonic plague, caused by the spread of the bacterium *Yersinia pestis* from rats to rat fleas to humans (not unlike how the bacterium that causes Lyme disease, *Borrelia burgdorferi*, is transmitted from rodents to deer ticks to humans). As a bacterium, *Y. pestis* is not known to enter cells through CCR5, or, in turn, to be blocked by CCR5 Δ32.

In another window, smallpox is offered as a competing narrative: like HIV, poxviruses enter white blood cells through chemokine receptors. And in yet another, a rebuttal: lethal smallpox did not become prevalent in Northern Europe until the 1600s—too late in history to have exerted sufficient selection pressure.

That view holds that the frequency of CC55 Δ32 in the present day can be explained by the plagues of the Middle Ages. While the Black Death was confined to a ~7-year period between 1346–1353 and spread throughout Europe, Asia, and the Middle East, the plagues of the Middle Ages persisted until 1670 and were confined to Europe. This series of plagues did not comprise re-occurrences of the bubonic plague, but of a viral hemorrhagic fever with a 100% mortality rate. In Northeastern Europe (and into West Asia), where there are the highest frequencies of CCR5 Δ32 today, hemorrhagic plague continued until 1800. People homozygous for CCR5 Δ32, immune to infection, survived and passed the allele on.

I find myself convinced by this study, perhaps because it is the easiest to understand.

But there is a chance the Black Death might not have been a bubonic plague. And even if it was, there is another window, another study, some in vitro macrophages from CCR5-deficient mice that showed a significantly reduced uptake of *Y. Pestis* compared to macrophages from wild-type mice. But the real mice all died.

I haven't even touched on the origin of the mutation, from when and whence it came. It might have been ~700 years ago, or ~2250. A large window. It might have been in Northern Europe, or it might have just been selected for there. The time and place the math arrives at depends on the model; change one part of the story and the whole story has to change.

Some say it was spread by the Vikings—who carried it east as they invaded and, less successfully, south.

~

Everyone in this poem is white. My uncle, me, my mother, my grandparents, the man or men he stayed with after running away probably, Tommy Tune, the TV stars I saw at tea, our ancestors. This troubles me: the fact of the frame.

In his email to my grandfather, my uncle described HIV as "a hideously stigmatic and selective disease," referring, I assume, to how it has disproportionately affected and been associated with gay men. But even when it was new and terrifying and he got it, it did not affect men who have sex with men alone. In the early 80s the CDC infamously labeled four groups as high-risk—the so-called "4-H Club": homosexuals, heroin users, hemophiliacs, and Haitians.

The virus itself, of course, has no prejudice; it does not discriminate.

Today, 1 in 2 black American gay and bisexual men will contract HIV in his lifetime. 1 in 11 white American gay and bisexual men will. The frequency of CCR5 Δ32 in white Americans is not high enough to explain this disparity.

~

                              How did you pay for treatment out of pocket?
You had your ways.
                              How did you know where to go?

A friend. A friend of a friend. Someone who knew someone who knew something.
                              How many of your doctors did you outlive?
Two, I think.

How did you know you had it at twenty-five,
in 1980—five years before the test was
developed and three before the virus had
been identified?
A flu that wasn't?

~

I should, at this point, explain the story of the Tommy Tune house.

Fire Island Pines is famous for its mid-century modern beach homes. Many of these were designed by Horace Gifford, the gay architect most closely associated with the minimalist cedar-and-glass aesthetic that became synonymous with the Pines. He died of AIDS in 1992.

___ Ocean Walk was built by Earl Combs, a contemporary of Gifford's, in 1968. According to the website of Pines Modern, an organization dedicated to preserving the architectural history of the Pines, Combs "engaged in tempestuous relationships with octagons" in his designs, best exemplified in ___ Ocean. He died of AIDS in 1991.

The main body of the house, which faces the Atlantic, is itself octagonal, as are the Ocean Walk-side entrance terrace, the master bedroom, the two terraces off the master suite, and all three rooftop terraces. The Pines Modern website accurately notes that the house's use of interior space is "spectacularly impractical," with a mostly open floor plan that contains just two bedrooms in three stories. Impractical but spectacular, yes: virtually every room (of which there are few) has ocean views. Upon its completion, the house was published in a 1969 issue of *House and Garden* in a story titled "Nine Suntraps on One Beach House."

Famously tall dancer and Broadway star Tommy Tune first visited the Pines in 1974 and bought ___ Ocean shortly after. He referred to the house, it's widely reported, as "the Emerald City done in cedar," a nod to its castle-like appearance from the beach. In 1984, Tommy Tune hired designer Michael

Gottfried to do a renovation, which was featured in *Architectural Digest* in 1985. Gottfried adjusted the height of the countertops and sinks to better match his client's tall frame, and decked out every reclinable surface with custom-fit white cushions. It was also during this renovation, I presume, that all the lights in the house were replaced with stage lights, a nod to Tune's other home on the Great White Way.

The lights aren't mentioned in any of the articles online, but I know about them because I'm staying here, and they're still hung, though many of the bulbs have now gone out, so that the house is always a little dark at night, even with all the switches flipped on.

In 2012, the house sustained serious damage during Hurricane Sandy. Most was exterior: the pool destroyed, the wooden walkway to the beach swept away, along with much (but not all) of the deck where Tommy Tune and Twiggy used to rehearse their dance numbers for the Broadway musical *My One and Only* on weekends away from the city. The house itself was okay, aside from a few leaks sprung in the roof, but from the beach—that view that once recalled the Emerald City—it does appear it's fallen "into disrepair," as the Fire Island Pines Historical Preservation Society describes it on their website.

Men walking by on the beach stop and stare at the thicket of broken beams in front of the house now, warped by water and wind into a twisted nest-like mess. Because image is everything in the Pines—each house and body and face carefully styled and maintained—the sight of something so unkempt makes for a spectacle of a different sort.

___ Ocean is not the only house that was ravaged by Hurricane Sandy, but it is one of only two houses that remain unrestored as of the time of my writing (summer 2017). Below a photo of the house from the 1980s posted by the Fires Island Pines Historical Society on Instagram, the comments read: "… alas now it's just a ruin, along with the house two doors down" "What's going on with those 2 homes ? It's been 5 years since Sandy" "Looks so good without the fucked up deck."

I have only met the current owner once, by accident, though I am catsitting for him this summer. There are three cats, all Siamese: one white with dark accents, one gray (what they call "blue") and one brown, who is my favorite, though I do my best not to let on. All three are unusually affectionate, all purrs and head rubs and attention-seeking. The brown cat who is my favorite is the most skittish of the three, but has always liked me, because, I like to think, we have a similar temperament. Hard to win over, but exceptionally sweet once you have.

When people ask me where I'm staying in the Pines—which is one of the first questions people ask in the Pines—I have to explain that I'm staying in the fucked-up Tommy Tune house on the beach, where I'm catsitting, alone. It's strange to be staying anywhere alone on Fire Island, as most houses are teeming with men—half- and quarter-shares and everyone's boyfriend or current trick—and just as strange to be staying in a dilapidated house, especially such a grand one on the beach. I call it the Grey Gardens of Fire Island Pines.

It's important to me to say, here, that I'm staying here for free, as though that absolves me of staying here, for free.

How, exactly, I came into caring for these cats I will have to leave a mystery, because it is someone else's story entirely, and, contrary to what this poem might suggest, there are some stories I will not tell.

~

Aarne-Thompson index type 326: The Boy Who Left Home To Find Out About the Shivers.

Kierkegaard: "In one of Grimm's fairy tales there is a story of a young man who goes in search of adventure in order to learn what it is to be in anxiety. We will let the adventurer pursue his journey without concerning ourselves about whether he encountered the terrible on his way."

~

At the memorial for you in Connecticut (your
friends held another in Florida), your
parents wouldn't let anyone talk about how
you died.

They were too old to travel when you were in
hospice; my mother was the only one in the
family who visited.

This was before your mother got sick the last
time, when she told me everything, and
before your father died, before the dementia
even. Before he used to call me Chris.[26]

~

Do you remember Laura Branigan's 1982 hit
"Gloria"?
They're playing a remix at tea, and I wonder how many times this song has
played in this harbor since it was new, how many men have danced to it and
shouted the words over the water, how many of them are dead.

Were you here? Did you like this song? Were
you happy? How? How long?
Why isn't anybody calling? I can't stop listening.

~

---

26   Did he? Did I know this? I don't remember it.

I first learned about CCR5 Δ32 in college, in an interdisciplinary seminar on biology and society that I took in order to fulfill the sole math-or-science requirement of my degree.

Though I demonstrated little care about my own sexual health as a teenager, I was interested in HIV/AIDS as a subject, and the unit on how activist responses to the crisis had challenged the medical establishment and shaped the course of research and medicine was my favorite that semester. We concluded by reading about the latest development in possible treatments: stem cell transplants from donors homozygous for CCR5 Δ32. Four years earlier, a man known as the Berlin Patient had undergone the procedure and been functionally cured of HIV.

Right away I thought of my uncle—dead five years but improbably alive so much longer—and of my great-grandmother, who was from Sweden, where the frequency of Δ32 of is ~14%, and of our other forebears, from Denmark and Germany and England, where it is ~12%.

I liked the idea of it, this blood amulet, I'm ashamed to admit. As if it could justify what little care I continued to pay.

~

This summer I received a fellowship for my writing, which felt something like winning the lottery, though the odds were better and the prize more modest. I used some of the money to buy an at-home DNA test dedicated to detecting the CCR5 Δ32 mutation.

I ordered the test the day the check came, but I haven't taken it, and won't. Human data collection is, I know, a nefarious business—DNA as evidence.

> And if I don't have it, the mystery of your life
> would remain.
> And if I do.

CCR5 Δ32, it turns out, is rarely what causes someone to be a long-term nonprogressor—what I imagined my uncle might have been, until he wasn't.[27] There is no answer there.

Instead I write this poem, which is an essay, which is a test, and in which there is no answer either.

~
~
~
~
~
~
~
~
~
~
~
~
~
~
~
~
~
~
~
~
~
~
~
~
~

---

27   He died because he stopped taking his medications.

Concluding Unscientific Postscript

Another memory:

Coming home from school in first or second grade and repeating what my best friend had said, that clogs are for fags.

My mom telling me that's a bad word, a bad word for gay people, you shouldn't say it, your Uncle Christopher is gay.

CCR5 Δ32 was first identified when I was six, the year this might have happened.
                    Let's say it was. 1996.
Something that has always been there is being discovered.

                    (Forgive me; I left more doors closed than I opened.)

How to Feel Good

There was the idea of love and then what.
Man Discovers Fire, Burns Self.
Practices losing weekends, months,
a season even, never enough not to be too much.
Like always wanting more cocaine
until the moment he wishes he'd done less,
the middle of the night is so short
and morning so long
when slept through. That's one solution.
Sex works best, probably,
but an excess of feeling can be exhausted.
I mean exhausting. I tried exercising
but I liked not exercising too much.
Poetry if you're hopeless,
novels if you like to feel smart,
though feeling smart only feels good
if you're not. Better not feel
too much or too little of anything
to feel good. Balance is recommended
unless you hate balance because, like me,
you have a personality disorder.
You might try TV.
Maybe don't have a personality disorder.
Self-care is hard but there's no comedown.
Walking helps, whatever else
they tell you in therapy.
No feeling is final, Rilke writes
in a poem about god I pretend isn't.
But you learned that already
on your way back up from the mirror,
from the burning, the whipping your head skyward,
the oh-god-why-can't-it-always-be-like-this.

There is no god, there is no reason.
Everything is as it should be,
which doesn't square politically but that's DBT.
You have to choose what to feel bad about.

Poem in Which Nothing Bad Ever Happens

It's however you would imagine it.
You specifically, whoever you are.
Whatever the precise conditions,
they are met. However you would
arrange the world, like a god or a
child, you can. It will last however
long as you can imagine it without
something going wrong. Not very.

A Poem for Pulse

Last night, I went to a gay bar
with a man I love a little.
After dinner, we had a drink.
We sat in the far-back of the big backyard
and he asked, What will we do when this place closes?
I don't think it's going anywhere any time soon, I said,
though the crowd was slow for a Saturday,
and he said—Yes, but one day. Where will we go?
He walked me the half-block home
and kissed me goodnight on my stoop—
properly: not too quick, close enough
our stomachs pressed together
in a second sort of kiss.
I live next to a bar that's not a gay bar
—we just call those bars, I guess—
and because it is popular,
and because I live on a busy street,
there are always people who aren't queer people
on the sidewalk on weekend nights.
Just people, I guess.
They were there last night.
As I kissed this man I was aware of them watching
and of myself wondering whether or not they were—just.
But I didn't let myself feel scared, I kissed him
exactly as I wanted to, as I would have without an audience,
because I decided many years ago to refuse this fear.
I left the idea of violence out on the stoop and went inside,
to sleep, early and drunk and happy.
While I slept, a man went to a gay club in Orlando
with two guns and killed forty-nine people.
Today in an interview his father said he had been disturbed
recently by the sight of two men kissing.

What a strange power to be cursed with:
for the proof of men's desire to move men to violence.
What's a single kiss? I've had kisses
no one has ever known about, so many
kisses without consequence—
But there is a place you can't outrun.
There will be a time when.
It might be a bullet, suddenly.
The sound of it. Many.
One man, two guns, fifty dead—
Two men kissing. Last night
I can't get away from, imagining it, them,
the people there to dance and laugh and drink,
who didn't think they'd die, who couldn't have.
How else can you have a good time?
How else can you live?
There must have been two men kissing
for the first time last night, and two women, too,
and two people who were neither.
Brown people, which cannot be a coincidence in this country
which is a racist country, which is gun country.
Today I'm thinking of the Bernie Boston photograph
Flower Power, of the Vietnam protestor placing carnations
in the rifles of the National Guard,
and wishing for a gesture as queer and simple.
The protester in the photo was gay, you know,
he went by Hibiscus and died of AIDS,
which I am also thinking about today because
(the government's response to) AIDS was a hate crime.
Reagan was a terrorist.
Now there's a president who names us,
the big and imperfectly lettered us, and here we are

getting kissed on stoops, getting married some of us,
some of us getting deported, some of us killed.
Here and there. Here and Over There.
We must love one another.
Violence is so rarely random.
Love can't block a bullet
but neither can it be shot down,
and love is, for the most part, what makes us.
We will be everywhere, always;
there's nowhere else for us, or you, to go.
Anywhere you run in this world, love will be there to greet you.
Around any corner, there might be two men. Kissing.

After the Reading

I know what it means
when the old poet says he liked
my more complex poems
even more I know which ones
he means the ones I read for him
not him specifically but
because of the fact of him
there the kind of him he is
if not the hegemonic him entire
one of its many heads

Those are good poems
I'm not sorry to read them
not sorry I'm not sorry
to read the ones he means
are simple the means
of which are simple the fact
of my him in plain language

which is not his kind
of him which has gone out
which has done his hitch
with multitudes of hims
A him like that is mis-
understood

I mean no disrespect
to this old house
I live in you
stand under your roof
and it is respectfully
I ruin you with my living

White Gays

Privilege is a man
taking up two seats on the train.
Now four, putting his feet up.

It is also my not having
to describe his leather loafers for you
to fill in the white space of his body
straight and able

and also my body's proximity
to his, across the aisle
on this train he is taking from
the Hamptons and I am taking
from the Pines. And how

at this distance
I can mistake my desire
for a greater difference
than it makes between us

—when my orientation is
to him, when his is the gaze
I've grown towards.

What I'm trying to see is this
proximity is the problem with White Gays.
How we now approach his station.

Proximity, because it promises
the possibility of arriving
where all the ease in the world
waits to be won.

Privilege is a tease, we forget,
what we learned in school.
Even spread in his lap,
everything for the taking
taken from someone.

Even this page
I claim, I claim.

Translator's Note on "I Woke Up"

Political[1] posing[2]—obviously[3] blond.[4]
Gender,[5] grieve[6] enabled.[7]

---

1   He was forced to leave his homeland for political reasons.
    In ideas those two political parties are worlds apart.

2   The model was posing carefully.
    She is always posing.

3   Obviously they were putting him to a severe test.
    Obviously he was lying.

4   Her long blond hair spilled down over her shoulders.
    This blond man delivers newspaper every morning.

5   The language differs from English in having gender for all nouns.
    Women are sometimes denied opportunities solely because of their gender.

6   Be sure and not grieve.
    What the eye does not see, the heart does not grieve over.

7   His photographic memory enabled him to tuck away yards of facts.
    Long practice enabled that American to speak fluently.

The Pines

Whoever they were,
I wasn't.

At the pool party, at seven,
at seventeen, if at twenty-seven

I haven't gotten in yet,
in my borrowed swimsuit,

legs dangling
over the edge of what

Matthew calls
dick soup.

It's his party, his suit,
his housemates

in the pool,
their friends and lovers

all glistening
gold and pink.

Like me, but
wetter. Like me

but not, somehow,
as it has always been

beginning in the family,
even in the face

of our shared face.
Even there.

And at the school,
where no one was like me,

and in the schoolyard,
where they made sure I knew it.

The girls liked me,
some of them, but I was stuck

a boy, distinct from them
as from the other boys.

Or I was the other boy.
Or I am the other

still, watching
from the blue periphery

as they flex and pose
for a photo

I am not in. But what
is the difference here

in this village of men
more or less

like me? More definition,
less poetry?

More muscle,
less mess?

A consciousness?
They are so happy

to be alike. That's all.
That's it.

The Tuck

Over tea (years ago) I told a friend
about the poem I was working on
thinking about a Schoenberg opera
and also Barthes and his theory of
waiting as a feminizing act—"Like
sort of a poem in drag"—I told her
but then began to worry that maybe
the premise was fundamentally sexist

though I have considered myself a
feminist since age fourteen and have
always strongly identified with female
protagonists—*The Little Mermaid*'s Ariel
for starters, and also (embarrassing)
Carrie Bradshaw, Glenn Close as Alex
Forrest in *Fatal Attraction*—I'M NOT
GONNA BE IGNORED, DAN—and

in the psych ward all my friends were
women, the men scared me, men do
scare me—walking alone past a group
of them at night I've always felt less
like them than like them—even when
I was very young I remember realizing
I'd be a better little girl than boy, push-
ing my penis down between my thighs

in the bath, making it disappear but then
the thing I like best in bed is being made
to feel like a man maybe because I don't
feel so attached to the idea the rest of
the time I'm just wandering around un-

tethered, without a shepherd, I'm a little
lamb who's lost in the wood—*Oh, Kay!*—
no I'm just swimming in this dress is all

A Question Looking at Men Looking at Women

It's wrong, I know.
Not the watching, but the wanting

to be the one watched: the woman,
if not the man who wants her,

who I want. I want him
to look at me

the way I catch him
look at her, subtle,

so as not to bother her
with his desire. But she notices.

Women do. Have to.
And I notice her noticing,

because I sit where I sit
opposite them in this subway car.

He asks for directions.
She gives them, returns

his smile and then,
still smiling, to her book.

It might be important to mention
he's handsome. The paint

on his boots. That I can't know
what it's like. He gets off first.

Men do. I watch her look
over the top of her book at him

looking back at her
as he exits, smiling to herself.

Every time someone I know
shows me she's

a woman, I'm jealous.
It's wrong, I know

gender isn't a question
of who's looking, but I don't know

what it's asking. What I am. All my life
I've thought about it.

All my life I've been thinking of men.

Craigslist Ode

To the young doctor, balding in Stuy Town,
and the straight boy from my school
I could never find on Facebook.
To the boy from the other college downtown,
with the good abs and the bad skin,
to the married guy in real estate who insisted
the sheets be fresh and liked to look into my eyes
the whole time he touched me. To that.
To the first one to reach for his wallet after,
somebody's father, and the first to tell me
a childhood secret. To the famous journalist
with the big dick I fell in love with,
and the baseball cap through the peephole
who said "this isn't going to work"
when I opened the door. To the guy
who held me down but wouldn't touch my dick,
to the redheaded bro in Murray Hill
whose dick smelled so awful. To my crush
from Hebrew class, to his name appearing
like a blessing in my inbox. To the guys
who used their real emails, bless them,
the guys whose girlfriends were out of town
or didn't give head or wouldn't wait up.
To the guys who'd never done this before.
To the liars. To the one who was older
than he said he was, to the one whose pictures
were old, to the one who tasted the way
old people smell but I did it anyway.
To the men who came from Queens
and Long Island and Jersey just to see me.
To the hairy guy with the yoga body,
the one with the muscles, the college wrestler

with the little dick. To the first one I took
money from, who was from Ireland,
and the second, who was from India,
to the guy on my block I felt bad for,
to the variety of religious undergarments
draped over my bookcase with care.
To the Looney Tunes boxers,
to the hemp necklace, to the fat gold ring,
to the appendectomy scar, to the old burn,
to the birthmark shaped like a country,
to the country it was shaped like,
to the gum removed and then stuck
to the windowsill, to these details
belonging to no one, to my ugly men
and my beautiful, all of them, the ones
unremembered even in metonymy,
my each and every who could have hurt me.

The Poem They Didn't Write

Was about how the company of women had constituted the best of their life.
Was a love song.
Advocated for platonic intimacy as the ideal form.
Quoted Plato quoting Socrates quoting Diotima.
Quoted Tim Dlugos telling Mary Ellen,
"I want to be a woman when I think / I could be like you."
Wondered: "Why have I already quoted men in a poem about my love of
     women?"
Quoted Cate:

>   "I don't want your face.
>   I want what your face can do."

Those lines were from the first thing they ever heard her read and they never
     forgot them.
The Poem They Didn't Write was about the brilliance of women,
their friends, how many of their most enduring relationships began
with the two of them recognizing the animal of the other in their poems.
Was about identification.
Reproduced Anna Swir's "The Same Inside" in full.
Whenever someone asked about their favorite poems they said
that one. Also: Anne Sexton's "Just Once." Also many poems by women
about men, but (just once) let's leave them out of this.
That's what's so great about the Swir poem,
how the encounter with the woman on the street replaces the need for the
     lover.
And how the encounter is not in fact a replacement but the real thing.
The lover is just a stand-in.
The Poem They Didn't Write always remembered that.
The Poem They Didn't Write began when they were dismayed
to realize they'd written a book about men.
In the Poem They Didn't Write, they felt free to say, "I'm not one."
The Poem They Didn't Write was an effort to correct
the image they saw reflected at the vanity.

In a meeting, Sampson (just one man) said it's strange, when he thinks of you
   he thinks of you in the company of women, but there aren't many in the
   poems.
Diana agreed, later over drinks, adding that it wasn't just about being friends
with mostly women, though it's true you were,
but also about how women were your strongest influences. Yes!
The Poem They Didn't Write would be an account of their literary education,
beginning with the Brontës and Mary Shelley, and include everything:
all their favorite writers, in the order they came to them,
and also their many brilliant friends and their greatest teachers
—Marie and Anne and Brenda and Deborah—
who also happened to be some of their favorite poets. What a lucky life!
they thought, working on the draft. It was also about the imperative to
"write like a man," which they had never understood or wanted to do,
though they had heard some of their brilliant friends confess this desire
in spite of themselves. They still couldn't figure out what it meant except that
perhaps the desire to "write like a man" was really just the desire to be read
like a man, which itself was really the desire not to be read like a woman.
Because of men.
        ("I don't want your face. / I want what your face can do.")
The draft was didactic but it felt like they were onto something.
They returned to their first idea for the Poem They Still Hadn't Written:
a personal history of feminine identification, in the form of a list.
They told Sasha about it as they waited for the play to start.
The Poem would begin with their mother, their childhood closeness,
with their stealing their older sister's dresses and library books,
which they used to read in a single sitting on the floor
of the downstairs bathroom, door locked.
        (A little girl named Alice lived in the mirror there.
        She and her world looked exactly like them and theirs, only she was
           a girl in hers.)

Then the Poem would turn to vignettes of adolescence:

Abby using an eyelash curler as a roach clip; Abby in oversized plastic
    sunglasses;
Abby passing them the roach and the sunglasses and then taking a picture;
the two of them searching her carpet for shake or scraping resin onto a piece
    of paper
when the town went dry, thanking Goddess when they remembered a nug
tucked away in a jewelry box; how hard they'd laughed, until they cried
or peed or begged the other to stop; each of them weeping, once,
in the arms of the other; sharing a bed. When they thought of
their happy times inside that unhappy time they thought of
her room, or ashing a Turkish Royal out the window in the back of Megan's
    car;
or later, when Abby got her license, packing the bowl in the passenger seat
as she drummed the wheel; or, once they got their license, the rides to school
with Sophie and Meg, seeing that terrible gay indie film
with Eryn instead of going to prom. They and Abby weren't speaking then.
And the soundtrack! They couldn't write the Poem They Didn't
without Joni and Carly and Stevie and Patti and Rickie and Liz
and Alanis and Fiona and Aimee and Chan and Regina and Rachael
and Corinne and Jenny and Joanna and Martha and and and
so the Poem They Didn't Write had to record something of the endless
exchange of mix CDs between Abby and them, their epic
reconciliation playlist, the nights the only plan was to lie back and listen.
Next the Poem followed them to New York, to parties with Martika
and bars with Seanne and concerts with both of them—
who liked some of the same music and had new voices to trade, too,
further nights to stay up smoking—
then to galleries with Dana and Sophia, after-after-parties.
But the list became monotonous: all coterie and no content.
They tried again. In a blank document they wrote
"Title: The One Boy at the Girls Sleepover" and nothing else.
They went to Athens with Elisa, who listened to them describe their struggle
and suggested they find a model. They thought about it until they thought of

Olena Kalytiak Davis's "The Poem She Didn't Write," from her book of the
     same title.
She'd visited when they were in grad school and led a master class.
The Poem They Didn't Write was a response to the prompt
she'd distributed, a worksheet titled
          "Irritable Reaching, _____, and the Psychology of Poetic Practice."
The Poem They Didn't Write reached irritably.
The Poem They Didn't Write was missing something.
The Poem They Didn't Write was not interested in psychology.
The Poem They Didn't Write missed analysis while they were in Greece.
They discussed gender a lot there—in analysis and in Athens, with Elisa.
It was a vexing question. They were asking.
But the Poem They Didn't Write wouldn't let that in, it was meant to be
a celebration, a praise song, simple and hummable, something children
     could sing
in a round, the girls and them at the sleepover.
The Poem They Didn't Write was about adoration, admiration, and only a
     little bit
about what they coveted (some new and perfect lines from Courtney
     crackling in their inbox).
The Poem They Didn't Write couldn't do their friends justice.
Was just a stand-in.
Tried, anyway.
Ended abruptly, with a recommendation:
          "This book is almost over. When you finish, please read Cate Mahoney,
          Diana Hamilton, Sasha Debevec-McKenney, Elisa Gonzalez, and
          Courtney Bush. May you find some joy in their company, as I do."

Story of My Life

Two desires, like twins I tend to:

the one to be
and the other to hold.

The first looks like envy,
when the brunette in cowboy boots cycles past
smoking a cigarette, her hair in a French braid.

She isn't sweating
like I am, through my shirt for the third time today.

She doesn't hurry.

Or later, in the park
where I am killing time, when the woman
on rollerblades shows me the shape

of what I sit on the edge of,
the same cobbled circle as always.

Looping and looping in a short dress.
Pixie cut. Perfect port de bras.
Her own music in her ears.

I read a book about a woman
who loves a man.
I relate. My own music.

Now the other desire cries out,
as though I can only neglect him for so long—

And there he is, this time
taking the form of a skateboarder
so lithe and dark-haired it hurts to look at him

though of course I can't stop,
knowing I'll have to go eventually, or he will,
and then I may never again have the pleasure

of looking at him. The pain I mean.
In my teeth.

I think of an Elaine Scarry line—
"The first demand of beauty is to keep looking"—

but when I go to look it up later, it's not there.

In fact, I wrote it, in my notes
on the book where I thought I'd find it,
the one about beauty and justice and error.

He's not very good.
At skateboarding, I mean:

he can't quite clear
the base of the statue that's drawn him here
and keeps tumbling away from his board.

Scarry says the first demand of beauty is replication.

I've already written this poem,
in this park, though it was a different statue
and a different man.

Is desire without pain possible?
Is desire possible without pain?

Really, I want to know.
I want to stop writing this poem.
I want him to say Yes.

And how graceful she is, avoiding his orphaned board
as it rolls her way.

Notes & Acknowledgments

The title of "Scintilla, Star" comes from a line in Derek Jarman's 1986 film *Caravaggio*.

The title of "Frantic Efforts to Avoid Abandonment, Real or Imagined" comes from *The Diagnostic and Statistical Manual of Mental Disorders* criteria for Borderline Personality Disorder.

"A True Account of Overhearing Andy Cohen at Fire Island" is after Frank O'Hara's "A True Account of Talking to the Sun at Fire Island."

"Short Essay on the Lyric-Conceptual Divide" is for Nick Vinocur.

"Oh," is for Wiley Birkhofer.

"Grasping at Being Filled" is after John Giorno's "Grasping at Emptiness," from which it takes its inspiration and form. It also borrows a line from Giorno's "AIDS Monologue."

In "Roughly," the statistics on the racial disparity in rates of new HIV infection in men in the U.S. come from Linda Villarosa's cover story for the June 11, 2017 edition of *The New York Times Magazine*, "America's Hidden HIV Epidemic." The Kierkegaard quote comes from Reidar Thomte's 1981 translation (in collaboration with Albert B. Anderson) of *The Concept of Anxiety*. In addition to the other sources named within the text, the poem draws on several scientific papers. These are:

Barmania, F., & Pepper, M. S. (2013). C-C chemokine receptor type five (CCR5): An emerging target for the control of HIV infection. *Applied & Translational Genomics*, 2, 3–16.

Clerici, M., Piacentini, L., Biasin, M., & Fenizia, C. (2009). Genetic correlates of protection against HIV infection: The ally within. *Journal of Internal Medicine*, 265(1), 110–124.

Elvin, S. J., Williamson, E. D., Scott, J. C., Smith, J. N., Pérez De Lema, G., Chilla, S., Clapham, P., Pfeffer, K., Schlöndorff, D., & Luckow, B. (2004). Evolutionary genetics: Ambiguous role of CCR5 in Y. pestis infection. *Nature*, 430(6998), 417.

Galvani, A. P., & Slatkin, M. (2003). Evaluating plague and smallpox as historical selective pressures for the CCR5-Δ32 HIV-resistance allele. *Proceedings of the National Academy of Sciences of the United States of America*, 100(25), 15276–15279.

Lopalco, L. (2010). CCR5: From Natural Resistance to a New Anti-HIV Strategy. *Viruses* (1999-4915), 2(2), 574–600.

Lucotte, G. (2001). Distribution of the CCR5 gene 32-basepair deletion in west Europe. A hypothesis about the possible dispersion of the mutation by the vikings in historical times. *Human Immunology*, 62(9), 933–936.

Mecsas, J., Franklin, G., Kuziel, W. A., Brubaker, R. R., Falkow, S., & Mosier, D. E. (2004). Evolutionary genetics: CCR5 mutation and plague protection. *Nature*, 427(6975), 606.

Novembre, J., Galvani, A. P., & Slatkin, M. (2005). The Geographic Spread of the CCR5 Δ32 HIV-Resistance Allele. *PLoS Biology*, 3(11), 1954.

Scott, S., Duncan, C. J., & Duncan, S. R. (2005). Reappraisal of the historical selective pressures for the CCR5-Δ32 mutation. *Journal of Medical Genetics*, 42(3), 205–208.

Solloch, U. V., Lang, K., Lange, V., Böhme, I., Schmidt, A. H., & Sauter, J. (2017). Frequencies of gene variant CCR5-Δ32 in 87 countries based on next-generation sequencing of 1.3 million individuals sampled from 3 national DKMS donor centers. *Human Immunology*, 78(11–12), 710–717.

I owe these researchers a great debt, as well as an apology for any misrepresentation or misinterpretation of their important work. My greatest debt in "Roughly," of course, is to my uncle and to my mother. I love you, Mom.

"A Poem for Pulse" is dedicated to the victims and survivors of the Pulse shooting.

After its original publication (as "I Woke Up"), "The Last Analysis; or, I Woke Up" was posted on the Chinese website enread.com. Seven words within the poem were footnoted with two examples of each used in a sentence. Those seven words make up the body of "Translator's Note"; the footnotes in my poem appear (almost) as-is.

"White Gays" refers to taking a train from the Pines. This train is actually leaving from the station in Sayville, Long Island, where the Pines Ferry is located.

In "How to Feel Good," DBT refers to Dialectal Behavioral Therapy.

The title of "A Question Looking at Men Looking at Women" is after the title of Siri Hustvedt's book *A Woman Looking at Men Looking at Women* and her essay of the same name.

"The Poem They Didn't Write" is after Olena Kalytiak Davis's "The Poem She Didn't Write."

*   *   *

I am grateful to the editors of the following publications, where these poems (sometimes in earlier versions or under different titles) first appeared:

After Dark: Grasping at Being Filled; Sometimes I See a Man Who Hurts Me
The American Poetry Review: Duplicity
The Believer: A Question Looking at Men Looking at Women; From a Friend; Oh,; Short Essay on the Lyric-Conceptual Divide
BOAAT: The Last Time I Got [ ]
b l u s h: After the Reading; Translator's Note on "I Woke Up"
The Brooklyn Rail: Craigslist Ode; I Don't Know Why, It Makes Me Sad; Poem in Which Nothing Bad Ever Happens; Strawberries
Cosmonauts Avenue: Poem in Which Nothing Bad Ever Happens to Me
Magma: The Tuck
The New Yorker: White Gays
Poetry: The Last Analysis; or, I Woke Up; Scintilla, Star
The Recluse: A True Account of Overhearing Andy Cohen at Fire Island; How to Feel Good; Selected Boys: 2003–2008
Washington Square Review: Frantic Efforts to Avoid Abandonment, Real or Imagined

"The Last Analysis; or, I Woke Up" was reprinted in *The Poetry Review*, *Gayletter*, and *Best New Poets 2017*.

"A Poem for Pulse" was included in the anthology *Bullets into Bells: Poets and Citizens Respond to Gun Violence*, edited by Brian Clements, Dean Rader, and Alexandra Teague.

*   *   *

Thank you to my editor, Sampson Starkweather, for his care and attention to this book, and to everyone at Birds, LLC for bringing it into the world. Thank you to Zoe Norvell for the cover and interior design, as well as to the Estate of George Paul Thek and the Alexander and Bonin Gallery for their permission to use Thek's painting for the cover.

Thank you to Courtney Bush, Elisa Gonzalez, Diana Hamilton, Cate Mahoney, and Sophie Robinson for the depth of their friendship and feedback on these poems.

Thank you to the faculty and staff of the NYU Creative Writing Program—especially Deborah Landau, Brenda Shaughnessy, and Jessica Flynn, for their steadfast encouragement—and to all my classmates there.

Thank you to BOFFO, the Pocantico Center, the New York State Council on the Arts, and the New York Foundation for the Arts for their generous support of my work.

Thank you to my family, for putting up with me. And to Jacques, for the same.

Finally, thank you to Dr. Arielle Freedberg, who helped me to find a life worth living. I would not have I come to everything else I did in these poems without you.